THE MANSION of MAZES

DAVID GLOVER

QED

Illustrator: Tim Hutchinson
Editor: Lauren Taylor
Designer: Maria Bowers
Language consultant: Penny Glover
Publisher: Zeta Jones

Quarto is the authority on a wide range of topics.

Quarto educates, entertains and enriches the lives of our readers—enthusiasts and lovers of hands-on living.

www.quartoknows.com

First published in hardback in the UK in 2011 by
QED Publishing
Part of The Quarto Group
The Old Brewery, 6 Blundell Street,
London, N7 9BH

A catalogue record for this book is available
from the British Library.

ISBN 978 1 84835 637 5

Printed in China

How to begin your quest

Are you ready for an amazing adventure – with twists and turns, exciting action and puzzles to solve? Then this is the book for you!

The Mansion of Mazes is no ordinary book – you don't read the pages in order, 1, 2, 3… Instead you must jump to and fro, forwards and back, as the plot unfolds. Sometimes you may lose your way, but the story will soon guide you back to where you need to be.

The story begins on page 4. Very soon you will have problems to solve and choices to make. The choices will look something like this:

If you think the correct answer is A, go to page 10

If you think the correct answer is B, go to page 18

Your task is to solve each problem and make the right choice. So, if you think the correct answer is A, you turn to page 10 and look for the symbol. That's where you will find the next part of the story.

But what happens if you make the wrong choice? Don't worry! The text will explain where you went wrong and send you back to try again.

The problems in this quest are all about shapes, space and measures. To solve them you must use your knowledge of lines, angles and measurements. To help you, there is a glossary of shape, space and measurement words at the back of the book, starting on page 44. You will find all the ideas you need there.

As you follow the quest you will be looking for clues to solve the mystery. You will make a note of the clues you spot in your detective's notebook. You will also collect different shapes and objects to put in the bag you are carrying. Try to remember the clues and the objects as you find them. You will need them all to complete the quest successfully.

So – do you think you are ready? Turn the page and let your adventure begin!

On a cold winter night, a 999 emergency call reports a crime at the Mansion of Mazes. Jewellery and paintings have vanished. There are footprints in the hall, but no signs of the burglars entering or leaving. The police are baffled and have asked you to solve the mystery. Are your detective skills up to the challenge?

When you arrive at the Mansion of Mazes, the moon is full. An owl hoots. You shiver and the door swings open. You step inside.

First, you must find the clues in the rooms and corridors. Shapes and patterns point the way. The clues will reveal the secret behind a cunning crime.

If you are ready for the challenge, go to page 28

If you are still not sure, go to page 32

You took the correct passage! Perpendicular means 'at a right angle', or 90 degrees. The other passageway was at a 45-degree angle to your direction.

Go to page 22

You take the left-hand passage. It's the correct passage! Soon it opens into a small building surrounded by trees. You recognize where you are. You are in the Mansion garden – not far from the front door.

You look back at the Mansion. You see a blaze of light in a window at the top of a turret.

Go to page 16

You have turned the wheel a whole turn. That's correct. One whole turn is 360 degrees. The pressure starts to fall and the boiler settles down.

Go to page 11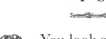

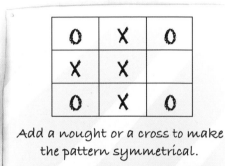

You look around the bedroom for more clues. You see a door next to the bed. The door is open a crack and you see the light is on. You open the door slowly and find yourself in a small bathroom. The basin is a mess. Someone has been using hair dye and hair clippers!

Then you see someone has been playing noughts and crosses in the steam on the bathroom mirror. There is a message underneath...

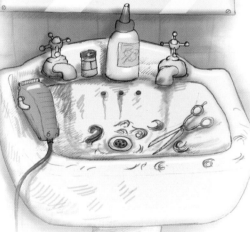

Add a nought or a cross to make the pattern symmetrical.

If you add a cross, go to page 23

If you add a nought, go to page 19

You open the cover. The pages have been cut to make a secret hiding place inside. There is a large iron key hidden in the space. This must be the key in the letter!
    You've chosen the correct book! You slip the key into your bag.

Go to page 13

You chose the correct weights! You add the flour until the scales are level.

Go to page 23

You open the door labelled 'Cellars'. You see the footprints going down the stairs. The burglars have been down there!

The way ahead is dimly lit by flickering light bulbs hanging on fraying wires. On the first step you find a ball of string resting on a note. You pick up the string and read the note...

Dear Detective,

These cellars are a maze. Follow the directions carefully. When you reach the boiler room, look for the shapes hidden there. You will need a shape with no flat faces and no edges to light your way. Watch out for clues along the way and use the string to help you find your way back.

Your Friend
PS Take care – the burglars have set Minotaur free!

You've heard of the Minotaur. It was a mythical beast. It had a man's body and a bull's head! But there can't be one down here, can there?

You tie one end of the string to the doorknob, and set off down the stairs. You unwind the string as you go. Soft footsteps follow close behind – but somehow you know they are friendly.

Go to page 12

You have chosen the correct direction! You walk along the passage. The air gets warmer. You hear the hiss of steam and the roar of flames. You must be heading for the boiler room. That's where the letter told you to go!

Go to page 27

You climb down the ladder into the dark. There are 20 rungs before you reach a cold stone floor – it's a good job you didn't fall! As you step off the ladder your foot touches something. It rolls away. You put your hand down and feel around – it's a torch! You press the button and the torch lights up the room. It's an amazing sight!

The trapdoor slams shut above you. Now you are trapped!

Go to page 30

You look around for the newly baked bread. The smell leads you into the larder where there is a pile of fresh loaves.

One of the loaves has a bite mark in it. The burglar could not resist eating the warm bread!

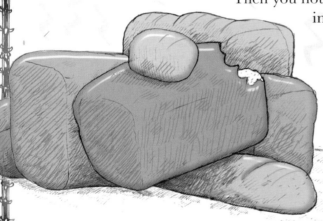

Then you notice something odd. There is a gap in the teeth marks. It's another clue! This burglar has a missing tooth! You take the piece with the teeth marks to use as evidence.

Go to page 39

The stone at the centre of the shape is loose. You pull it out with your fingertips. Someone has hidden a slip of paper in the space behind. There is something written on it.

It's the title of a book! But what does E,5 mean?

Go to page 20

Through the Looking Glass

By Lewis Carroll

E,5

7

You turn to the right by less than a right angle, but suddenly come to a dead-end. You turn around. A dog with huge jaws and glowing green eyes blocks your path. It's Minotaur, the bull-mastiff! Then you hear growling from behind you. Minotaur looks nervous. The growling gets louder until Minotaur runs away.

You chose the wrong direction. An obtuse angle is between 90 degrees and 180 degrees. You turned less than 90 degrees – that's an acute angle. You follow the string back to the turning point.

Go to page 34

You set off along the passage. Soon you see footprints. You are going in the right direction! At the end of the passage you find a door. It opens onto a spiral staircase. You saw the light at the top of the turret, so you climb up.

You're getting so used to all this maths that you decide to count the stairs as you climb. There are exactly 28. The staircase ends at another door. There is a note pinned to the wood. You read it carefully...

Dear Detective,

Each door in this tower has a name. The number of steps you climb to reach the door is the clue to which handle to pull.

Your Friend

There are two handles on the door, one labelled January, the other February.

If you turn the January handle, go to page 42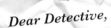

If you turn the February handle, go to page 41

You look around for clues. Then you see patterns carved around the fireplace. They are not as dusty as the rest of the room. Someone has been touching them! You step closer. The patterns are triangles! Is one of them an equilateral triangle?

If you think triangle A is equilateral, go to page 38

If you think triangle B is equilateral, go to page 39

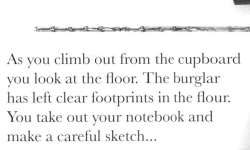

As you climb out from the cupboard you look at the floor. The burglar has left clear footprints in the flour. You take out your notebook and make a careful sketch...

There are some paw prints as well!

Now you have located the jewels in the kitchen, and found the teeth marks in the bread, you must look for clues in other parts of the Mansion. You head back to the Grand Hall as fast as you can!

Go to page 15

You reach step 365 and stop. There is a door on your left. This must be it! You listen for a moment. There are voices inside!

Taking a deep breath you open the door and step through. Barkimedes is by your side.

Go to page 43

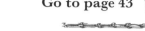

You look around for some salt. You see three shakers on a shelf. There is a note next to them...

The salt is in the shaker that rolls but will not roll away. Make sure you choose the right one!

cylinder   cuboid   cone

You decide to see how the shapes roll. You try the cuboid first. You lay it on its side but it will not roll at all. Then you try the cylinder and the cone. One of them rolls in a straight line away from you. The other rolls around in a circle and comes back!

If you think the salt is in the cylinder, go to page 38

If you think the salt is in the cone, go to page 34

You press the shapes in the order 2, 3, 1. Nothing happens, so you press harder. Suddenly the trapdoor gives way. You are falling into a dark pit! At the last minute strong teeth grab your shoes. You are dragged back from the danger. The trapdoor swings up and slams shut.

You pressed the shapes in the wrong order. The area is the amount of surface a shape covers. When a shape is drawn on a grid you can find its area by counting the squares it surrounds.

Go to page 21

You look around the rest of the boiler room. In one corner you see a stack of thin parcels wrapped with brown paper. Are they the stolen paintings?

You look closely at the parcels. You recognize some of the shapes, but there are too many! Then you find a note on one of the parcels...

Dear Detective,

The burglars have hidden the stolen paintings with some fakes. One of the burglars will be back soon to move the paintings to another hiding place. You must take the genuine paintings and hide them now. Hurry!

Your Friend

You look back at your notebook for the shapes of the paintings. You've written 'square, rectangle, hexagon, octagon'.

If you take these shapes, go to page 39

If you take these shapes, go to page 20

You start to take down the books from shelf X. The fourth one you open is *Through the Looking Glass* – you chose the correct shelf!

Go to page 26

The room is empty! The sound of voices is coming through an air vent. The door slams behind you.

Then you hear a rumble. The stone floor is sliding to one side. There is a pit of fire below. Soon you will fall into it! Quickly you take the pyramid from your bag. You jam one edge into the crack between the floor and the wall – perhaps it will work as a wedge? With a groan and a creak the floor stops moving. Now you must escape. Barkimedes spots a way out. He grabs a loose plank in the door with his jaws and pulls it free. You both crawl through the gap.

There are 366 days in a leap year. How many days in a normal year?

Go to page 37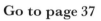

After a few steps the passage splits in two. Which way should you go? Then you see a message chalked on the wall...

Take the passage that is perpendicular to yours.

Go to page 42

Go to page 4

You came this way

You have taken the right direction. An obtuse angle is between 90 degrees and 180 degrees. The other direction was less than 90 degrees to your tunnel – that's an acute angle.

Go to page 15

Now you have the key you must find the 'ancient shape'. What can it be? You look around the library for more clues.

There is a large desk in the centre of the room. It is covered with drawings and plans. You take a closer look. One plan seems to be for the library you are standing in! Someone has scribbled a note in one corner...

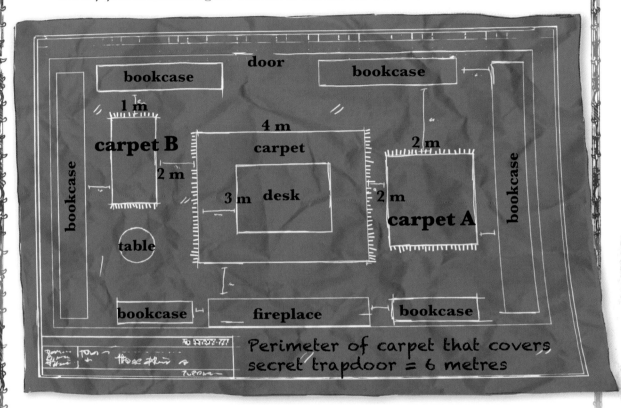

Perimeter of carpet that covers secret trapdoor = 6 metres

There is a secret trapdoor! Something important could be hidden there. And the plan shows all the carpets in the room. Which one should you look under to find the trapdoor?

If you think the trapdoor is under carpet A, go to page 40   **If you think the trapdoor is under carpet B, go to page 18**

You've set the clock to the wrong time! Its alarm starts to sound loudly. The burglars will hear it! Quickly, you take a pillow from the bed and muffle the sound until it stops. '1:30' is the same as 'half-past one'.

Go to page 18

Cautiously, you reach forwards and open the lid. Inside is a mummy wrapped in bandages. Its eyes glow red. Its bony hands reach out to grab your neck. It's going to pull you inside!

Suddenly the mummy case slams shut. Someone has pushed the door – there are paw marks on it! The mummy is trapped inside again.

You chose the wrong case. This is the net for a prism, not a pyramid.

Go to page 36

 You look around. Then you see a set of kitchen scales on a table. Next to it is a bag of flour, and a floury hand print on the table top. The hand that made the print has a scar! You sketch the print in your notebook.

Someone has left a list of instructions on a scrap of paper next to the flour. You decide to follow the instructions to work out what they were doing!

1. Weigh out exactly 0.5 kg of flour.

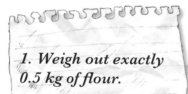

If you think this set of weights adds up to 0.5 kg, go to page 6

If you think this set of weights adds up to 0.5 kg, go to page 40

You see suspicious footprints on the floor. They lead off in four directions. Where should you investigate? Then you hear a floorboard creak. The sound came from the top of the stairs!

Library,
go to page 35

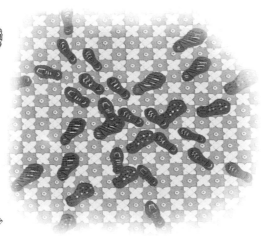

Kitchens,
go to page 29

Cellars,
go to page 6

Main staircase,
go to page 21

The passageway ends at a door labelled 'Candle Store'. You turn the handle and enter. The storeroom is packed with candles on shelves.

　　You remember the note at the top of the cellar stairs said, 'You will need a shape with no flat faces and no edges to light your way.' It could be a candle! But which will you choose?

cylindrical candles

conical candles

spherical candles

polyhedral candles

If you take a spherical candle, go to page 22

If you take a cylindrical candle, go to page 41

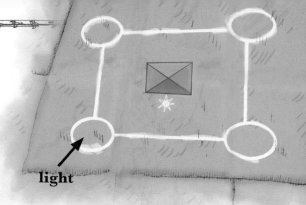
light

 Which turret was that? You will need to know when you go back inside. Then you see a design on the stone floor of the garden building. It's a plan of the Mansion. At the centre of the Mansion there is a square hole with triangular sides. Against one side there is a picture of the sun.

Of course! It's the sun from the pyramid! The hole is a pyramid shape! You take the pyramid from your bag, turn it upside down and drop it in the hole making sure the sun is on the correct side. A diagram on the base of the pyramid shows the points of the compass. Now you can tell which turret is which!

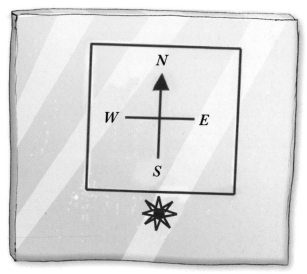

If you think the light is in the south-west turret, go to page 42

If you think the light is in the north-west turret, go to page 28

 You reach step 366 and stop. There is a door on the right. This must be it! You listen for a moment. There are voices inside!

Taking a deep breath you open the door and step through. Barkimedes is with you.

Go to page 12

16

That's too much water! As you lift the jug, its handle snaps. It had been partly cut through! The jug shatters. The water seeps between the flagstones on the kitchen floor. Ivy starts to grow from the cracks. It wraps around your ankles – you are trapped! Then you feel strong jaws grab your belt and pull. You break free from the tendrils. Quickly, you sprinkle salt on the ivy leaves, and they shrink back.

There are 1000 ml in a litre. So 250 ml is less than ½ litre. What fraction of 1000 is 250?

Go to page 32

You step through the doorway into the hiding place. It's a tiny room with walls made from stone blocks. There is a stool in the centre. On the stool is a note...

> *Dear Detective,*
>
> *The next clue is at the centre of a hexagon.*
> *Your Friend*

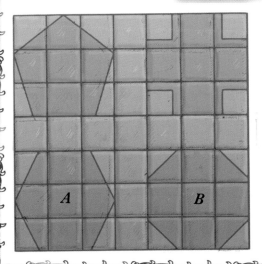

You sit on the stool and look around. Someone has scratched lines on the walls – perhaps centuries ago when they were hiding from highwaymen! The lines make shapes around the stones.

If you think stone A is at the centre of a hexagon, go to page 7

If you think stone B is at the centre of a hexagon, go to page 27

You roll up carpet B. There is a trapdoor in the floor beneath! You chose the correct carpet. Its perimeter is 2 m + 1 m + 2 m + 1 m = 6 m.

Go to page 21

 That's the correct time! The clock was stopped at a quarter past nine. Then you see a note on the mantelpiece. You read it carefully...

Dear Detective,

Reset the clock to the correct time. The burglars have set it to the wrong time to confuse you!

Your Friend

You look at your watch to see the time now...

If you set the clock like this, go to page 35

If you set the clock like this, go to page 13

You have chosen the correct bowl. Its diameter is 30 cm, so its radius is 15 cm. You read the next instruction...

Go to page 10

3. Add a sprinkle of salt, some yeast, and 250 ml of water to the flour in the bowl.

As you leave the Candle Store you see another note pinned to the door. You study the directions on the note...

Dear Detective,

The next passage you need is parallel to the one along which you came. Turn left. Then turn again to find it.

Your Friend

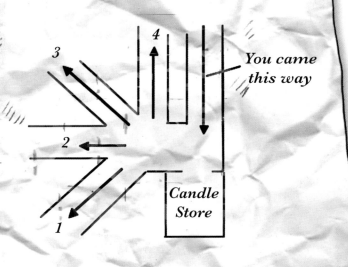

You leave the Candle Store, turning left out of the door. Soon you come to a space with passages leading in four directions, just as the note said you would. Which one is parallel to the passage along which you came?

If you take passage 4, go to page 6

If you take passage 2, go to page 38

As you add a nought to the pattern, the bathroom begins to fill with steam. The taps gush scalding water. You can't turn them off! The door is locked – you cannot escape! Then there is a loud crash. It's Barkimedes! He has broken through the door. He has a large spanner in his mouth. You use the spanner to turn off the taps.

Adding the nought did not make the pattern symmetrical. There are now more noughts on the right than on the left.

Go to page 5

You start to tell the man and woman to call the police, but Barkimedes barks fiercely. The man and the woman back into a corner.

Look again at the clues. The man who is standing has a missing button and a scar on his hand. The pattern on his shoe matches the one in the flour. His accomplice, the cook, has a gap in her teeth!

Go to page 43

A loud barking noise warns you that something is wrong. You have not picked up all the real paintings! Quickly you replace the fake paintings.

This shape is a trapezium, not a hexagon. A hexagon has six sides.

This shape is a pentagon, not an octagon. A octagon has eight sides.

Go to page 11

You step back into the library. Now you must find the book. There are thousands of them! They are so old and dusty you can't read the titles on their spines. Finding *Through the Looking Glass* is going to take forever!

Then you see that the bookcases and shelves are marked with letters and numbers. Some are so worn you cannot read them, but you can work out where E,5 is!

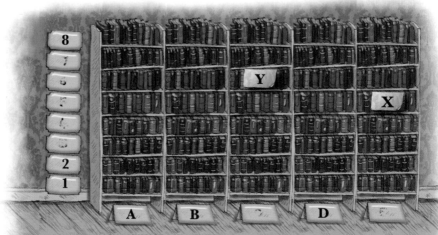

If you think E,5 is shelf X, go to page 11

If you think E,5 is shelf Y, go to page 22

The trapdoor does not have a handle. It is made from squares of wood –
like a chess board. Some of the squares are coloured to make patterns.
Then you spot a message scratched into the floorboards...

*To open the trapdoor you must press the
shapes in order of their area – smallest
first. Make sure you do not make a
mistake, or you may get a surprise!*

If you press the shapes in
order 2, 3, 1, go to page 10

If you press the shapes in
order 2, 1, 3, go to page 37

You run up the stairs. On the top step you find a scribbled note...

Dear Detective,

*Do you have the key? Have you found
the paintings and the jewels? If not, go no
further, or all will be lost!*

Your Friend

If you have found the key,
paintings and jewels,
go to page 35

If you haven't found the
key, paintings and jewels,
go to page 15

You take a spherical candle from the shelf. You step back through the door. Suddenly all the lights in the passage fail! But a flame appears on your candle. It lights your way – just as the letter said it would!

You were right. A sphere has no flat surfaces or edges. Its surface is a smooth curve all over.

Go to page 19

 The passage soon divides again – this time in three directions. There is another set of instructions pinned to the wall...

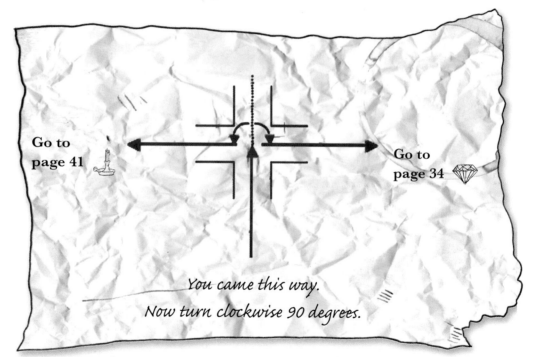

Go to
page 41

Go to
page 34

You came this way.
Now turn clockwise 90 degrees.

 You reach up to take the books down from shelf Y. As you pull out the first book, a loud bark makes you jump to one side. The bookcase topples and crashes to the floor – just where you had been standing. That was close! Where did that bark come from?

You chose the wrong shelf. The E and the 5 are coordinates. Count along the book cases A, B, C, D, E. Count up the shelves 1, 2, 3, 4, 5.

Go to page 20

You read the next instruction...

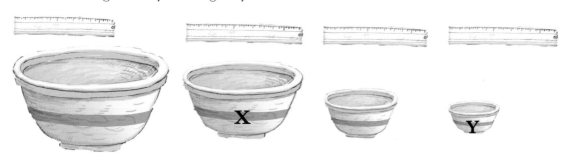

*2. Put the flour in a
bowl. Use the bowl
with a radius of 15 cm.*

There is a row of bowls – all different sizes – high on a shelf. But which is the 15 cm radius bowl? Then you remember your school ruler is 30 cm long. You try to imagine your ruler next to each of the bowls.

**If you lift down bowl X,
go to page 18**

**If you lift down bowl Y,
go to page 37**

A cross is correct! The pattern looks the same if you turn it by 90 degrees or 180 degrees, or look at it in a mirror. As you add the cross, steam starts to clear from the mirror. Another message is revealed...

Dear Detective,
Clothes and hair dye
may disguise,
But don't be fooled
by burglars' lies!
Now follow me to the turret,
To put an end to this crime!
Your Friend

Barkimedes leads the way. Together you follow the burglars' footprints from the bedroom into the passage. The passage twists and turns. You pass dozens more rooms, but they are all empty. The passage finally ends at an old wooden door, leading to the turrets.

The door is locked! But you have the old iron key.

Go to page 33

Now it is the criminals' turn to be tied up. While you phone the police station and gather the stolen goods as evidence, the owner leads the butler and the cook into the Grand Hall and ties them to two chairs. Barkimedes growls at them angrily – they are too scared of him to try and escape!

The owner smiles when he sees his belongings safe and sound.

"I can't thank you enough," he says. "Some of these things have been in my family for generations – they are priceless to me."

Barkimedes barks happily and wags his tail. You crouch down to pat him on the head. You are not the only one to thank – you couldn't have done it without Barkimedes.

"You may need a new butler and cook," you say. "But you'll never need another dog!"

THE END

Inside the cover of *Through the Looking Glass*, you find a folded sheet of paper. It's another clue!

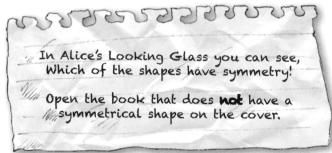

In Alice's Looking Glass you can see,
Which of the shapes have symmetry!

Open the book that does **not** have a
symmetrical shape on the cover.

You look at the first three books you took down. Each has a shape on the cover. Which shape is not symmetrical? That's the book you must open.

A   **B**

You can see that each side of the heart would look identical if held against a mirror. It has a line of symmetry down the middle. The left half is a mirror image of the right. But which of shapes A and B is not symmetrical?

If you open book A, go to page 29

If you open book B, go to page 5

You have saved the paintings! But there is still much to do. There are burglars to catch!

The secret door opens again as you push it. You begin to follow the string to find your way back. As you pass the boiler room you see something shining on the floor. It's a silver button. It could be another clue! You pop it in your pocket, and follow the string all the way back to the entrance hall.

Go to page 15

The stone at the centre of the shape is loose. You pull it out with your fingertips. In the dark space behind you see a pair of bright eyes and the flicker of a forked tongue. There's a snake in there! Quickly, before the snake can strike, you push the stone back.

You chose a shape with eight sides – that's an octagon. How many sides does a hexagon have?

Go to page 17

The boiler room door is open. It's very hot inside. The fire is blazing inside the furnace. Hot steam pipes rattle and hiss. The pressure gauge shows danger – the boiler is about to explode!

You see a notice on the boiler wall...

In an emergency, turn the valve wheel 360 degrees. This will release the pressure.

If you turn the wheel until it looks like this: **go to page 43**

If you turn the wheel until it looks like this: **go to page 5**

27

You set off along the passage and spot another door. It must lead into the turret. You open it, but there is no floor! You start to topple over into empty space. But Barkimedes grabs your shirt with his teeth and pulls you back.

You took the wrong passage. With the compass points facing this way, turret Y is to the north-east.

Go to page 33

That's the wrong turret! If you go there you will waste too much time.

Go to page 16

 You are in the Grand Hall. There is a small table in front of you. On it is a letter addressed to you!

> *Dear Detective,*
>
> *I need your help to catch the burglars. You must find the clues that will trap them. I have left notes to help you. First try to find the stolen items. But take care – the burglars have set traps for you!*
>
> *Your Friend*

You look around and see shapes on the walls where priceless paintings once hung – now they have been stolen. You make a note of the shapes in your notebook. They might be important!

square   **rectangle**   **hexagon**   **octagon**

Go to page 15

The footprints lead you down a flight of steps to a large door labelled 'Kitchens'. The smell of fresh bread wafts through the door. Then you hear something – it sounds like an animal licking its lips! The kitchens are huge. There is a great open fireplace. There are banks of ovens, huge wooden tables and racks of pots and pans. Just inside the door is a notice board with meal times and menus. Someone has pinned up a letter addressed to you!

Dear Detective,

The burglars have hidden some of their loot in here! Measurements and a recipe will show you where to look. In your search, look for a bite with something missing. You will need it to solve the crime!

Your Friend

Go to page 14

You open the book. The pages have been cut to make a secret space inside. There is something in there. It's a giant centipede! It starts to crawl towards your hand. Then a loud bark makes you jump into action. You slam the book shut.

You chose the wrong book! The face is symmetrical. It has a line of symmetry like the heart (hold page 26 up to a mirror to check).

Go to page 26

You are in a store room under the library. There are boxes of books, and cabinets filled with strange objects – a telescope, a brass microscope and other ancient scientific instruments. Everything is covered with cobwebs.

In one corner you see a set of mathematical shapes on a shelf.

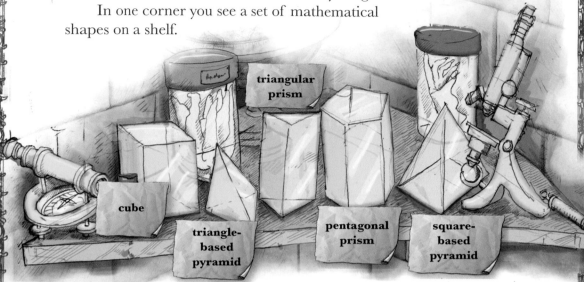

You remember the description in the letter, 'an ancient shape with 5 faces and 8 edges'. Perhaps one of these is the shape you need? You start to count the faces and edges. You record the numbers in a table in your notebook...

Shape	Number of faces	Number of edges
Cube	6	12
Triangle-based pyramid	?	?
Triangular prism	5	9
Pentagonal prism	7	15
Square-based pyramid	?	?

The first three shapes you check don't have the correct number of faces and edges. What about the two that are left?

If you think you need a triangle-based pyramid, go to page 42

If you think you need a square-based pyramid, go to page 36

You have measured correctly! As you stir in the water, the mixture becomes soft and rubbery. It's bread dough! That must be the clue. You remember smelling baking bread. Someone had been baking just before you arrived. It must have been the burglars, but why would they bake bread in the middle of a robbery?

Go to page 7

 Very soon the passage divides. Which way should you go? Then you see someone has chalked a message and a shape on the wall.

Look for this shape. It will take you to safety.

You shine your torch along the two passageways. There is a pile of blocks in each one. The piles are turned compared to your drawing. But one of them must have the blocks in the same pattern – which will you choose?

Left

If you choose the left passage, go to page 4

Right

If you choose the right passage, go to page 34

Don't be afraid. Help is always nearby. When you are stuck, a mysterious helper will guide you. Just follow the instructions one at a time, and see how far you get. Now make your way to the Grand Hall to begin your adventure. Good luck!

Go to page 28

Now you need some water. There are plenty of taps over the sinks, but how will you measure 250 ml? You see a measuring jug. That's what you need! The jug has a scale. It is marked 1 litre at the top, but the only other markings are fractions. Luckily you think you know how many millilitres there are in a litre. So you fill the jug to the correct level.

If you fill the jug like this, go to page 17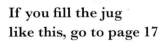

If you fill the jug like this, go to page 31

The clues confirm the truth! The burglars have captured the owner and tied him up! As Barkimedes stands guard over the two criminals you untie the prisoner.

　　　The owner explains the burglars' plot. The butler and the cook were going to keep him prisoner in the cellar. The butler would pretend to be him when the police came. After the police had failed to solve the crime, the criminals would take the paintings and jewellery from their hiding places, and make their getaway!

Go to page 24

You take the key from your bag and fit it in the keyhole. It's stiff but you manage to turn it. A short flight of steps climbs to a circular room. Four passageways lead from the room at right angles to each other.

The passages lead to the turrets! But which is which? Then you see it! There is a pyramid-shaped hole at the centre of the floor. Just like the one in the garden! You take the pyramid from your bag and drop it into the hole with the sun picture on the correct side. Now you can go to the correct turret! Which do you choose?

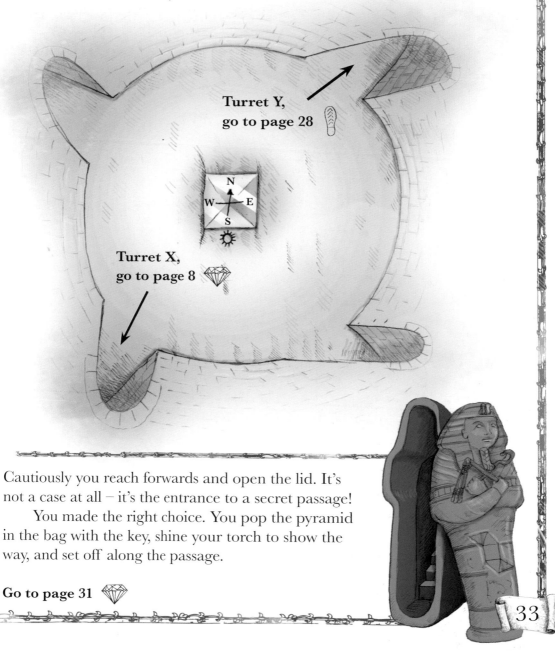

**Turret Y,
go to page 28**

**Turret X,
go to page 8**

Cautiously you reach forwards and open the lid. It's not a case at all – it's the entrance to a secret passage!

You made the right choice. You pop the pyramid in the bag with the key, shine your torch to show the way, and set off along the passage.

Go to page 31

You take the right-hand passage. It is steep and slippery. Your shoes lose their grip. You start to slide, dislodging small pebbles along the way. Then something grabs your collar and pulls you back to safety. You hear the pebbles splash into a deep underground pool – that could have been you!

You chose the wrong shape. Try to turn the shapes in your mind to match the one in the drawing. Look at the block at the top of the shape – that will help you.

Go to page 31

 It's the correct direction. But soon the passageway splits again – this is giving you a headache! There are more instructions taped on the wall.

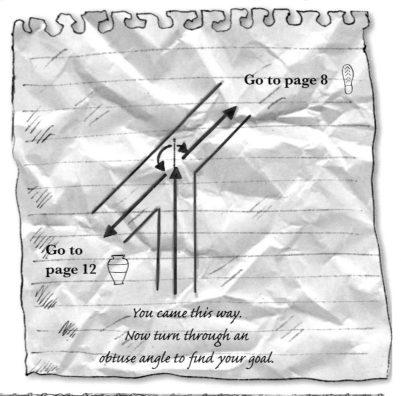

Go to page 8

Go to page 12

You came this way.
Now turn through an
obtuse angle to find your goal.

 You shake the cone over the flour bowl. It's the right shaker. A sprinkle of salt falls onto the flour. A cone rolls in a circle when you lay it on its side

On the shelf next to the shakers you see a jar labelled 'yeast'. You add a spoonful of that to your mixture, too.

Go to page 32

You step through the library doors. Suddenly it feels cold. The wind whistles down the chimney. You start to feel scared. But then you hear a friendly woof. You feel better again.

You check the windows. They are locked. The burglars could not enter or leave that way. Then you spot the safe. It's open! The jewels it held have been stolen with the paintings! A note left inside the safe tells you what to do...

> Dear Detective,
> You must find a key and an ancient shape with five faces and eight edges. An equilateral triangle is the first clue.
>
> Your Friend

Go to page 9

That's correct! As you move the hands to the correct time, it starts to tick.

Go to page 5

Suddenly you realize a large friendly dog is bounding up the stairs with you. It's Barkimedes the bloodhound. The Mansion is his home, and he's been helping you all along!

On the first-floor landing there are rows of doors. All are closed apart from one. You step inside. It's the owner's bedroom! The burglars have been in and stolen some of his clothes! Why would they do that? In their hurry they seem to have knocked the clock from the table.

If you think the clock stopped at a quarter past nine, go to page 18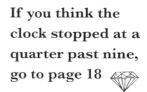

If you think the clock stopped at a quarter to three, go to page 40

You pick up the square-based pyramid. It's heavy in your hand. You turn it around. There is a picture of the Sun and a message on one face.

*You need me
to solve a vital clue,
But first you have to
leave this room.
A mummy's case
is the door for you.
My net will show
you what to do.*

It doesn't make sense! You understand that you will need the pyramid later on, but what's all that about a mummy's case and a net?

You look desperately around. Then your torch shines on two large objects against the wall. They are Egyptian mummy cases! Egyptian mummies were placed inside them in the pyramids!

You walk over to the mummy cases. They have strange symbols on the front. You recognize the symbols! They are mathematical nets. If you draw them on card, you can cut them out and fold them to make solid shapes! One must be the net for a pyramid. That's the one you need.

**If you choose the red
mummy case, go to page 14**

**If you choose the blue
mummy case, go to page 33**

As you lift the bowl from the shelf you look inside. A row of shiny white eyes stares back! It's a huge poisonous spider! A loud bark makes you drop the bowl. It shatters. The spider scuttles behind the sinks.

You chose the wrong bowl! The radius of a circle is half its diameter. Bowl Y has a diameter of 15 cm, so its radius is 7.5 cm.

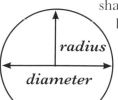

Go to page 23

The room is empty! There is just a lamp standing on a table next to a hastily written letter...

Dear Detective,

I have tracked the burglars to their hiding place. They are deep underground behind the 'Days of the Year' door! You must count the stairs carefully as you descend. The 'Leap Year' door leads to danger!
Hurry — I need your help!

Your Friend

As fast as you can you race down the stairs, counting as you go... *three hundred and sixty, three hundred and sixty one, three hundred and sixty two...*

If you stop at step 365, go to page 10

If you stop at step 366, go to page 16

It's the correct sequence. The trapdoor swings smoothly up to reveal a dark hole. There is an iron ladder going down below.

Go to page 7

You press triangle A. A blast of flame roars from the fireplace! Strong teeth grab your belt and pull you to safety. Who was that?

It was the wrong triangle. An equilateral triangle has three equal sides and three equal angles. Triangle A has only two equal sides and angles. The third side and angle are different from the others. It is an isosceles triangle.

Go to page 9

isosceles triangle   *equilateral triangle*

You shake the cylinder over the flour bowl. It's pepper, not salt. But this is not ordinary pepper – it is extra strong! Your eyes are watering, your nose running and your mouth burning. You think your head will explode! Then something pushes you to the sinks – you need to wash the pepper away. You hold your head under a running tap until you feel better.

A cylinder rolls in a straight line when you lay it on its side.

Go to page 10

You set off along passage 2. It gets colder the further you go. There is a door at the end marked 'Ice Store'. You open it and look inside. The walls and ceiling are covered in frost. Then the door slams behind you. You hear the key turn in the lock! You are trapped! You will freeze!

Then you hear paws scrabbling at the door. The key drops to the floor with a clang. It is pushed under the door so you can escape!

You chose the wrong direction. When two directions are parallel they are the same distance apart at every point and never meet.

You follow your string back along the passageway.

Go to page 19

You see fingerprints on triangle B, so you press it. The bookcase to the right of the fireplace swings open. It's a secret door. There is a hiding place behind the wall. You made the right choice!

Go to page 17

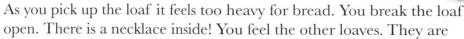

As you pick up the loaf it feels too heavy for bread. You break the loaf open. There is a necklace inside! You feel the other loaves. They are heavy, too. That's how the burglars have hidden the jewels!

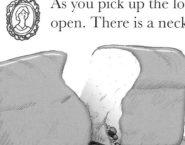

Then you hear footsteps in the corridor. One of the burglars is coming back. Quickly you hide the broken bread under the other loaves. You spot a cupboard where you can hide, but before you get inside, you sprinkle flour on the floor.

Go to page 43

You have taken the correct paintings! You run from the boiler room with them in your arms. You hear heavy footsteps coming down the passageway. Which way should you go? Then you hear a scraping sound. A hidden door is opening in the wall! You feel afraid and turn to run, but strong teeth grab you from behind. They pull you through the door.

You are in a small room filled with precious china, silver plates and candlesticks. This is where the Mansion's valuables are kept! It's a great place to hide the paintings.

Then you hear an angry shout. The burglar has discovered the paintings are gone! He or she runs back the way they came – you hear footsteps disappearing into the distance.

Go to page 26

You start pouring the flour. The scales tilt with a jerk. Someone has tied a string to one pan – it's a trap! The string pulls a jar of oil from a shelf onto an oven. The jar shatters. The oil catches fire! You must not put water on an oil fire – it will spread! Then a bark makes you turn. You see a fire blanket next to the ovens. You grab it and spread it over the flames. The flames go out.

There are 1000 g in a kg, so 0.5 kg is 500 g, not 50 g.

Go to page 14

You roll up carpet A. Strange fumes start to rise from between the floorboards. You are passing out! Then something pushes the carpet back into place. You feel a wet tongue lick your face, and you come around.

You chose the wrong carpet! The *perimeter* is the distance all the way around the shape. The diagram below shows how to calculate the perimeter of the carpet. Try this with carpet B.

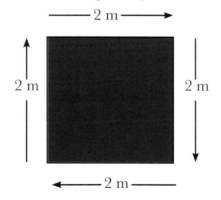

Perimeter =
2 m + 2 m + 2 m + 2 m = 8 m

Go to page 13

That's the wrong time! The big hand shows the minutes and the little hand the hours. The little hand is on the nine. The big hand is pointing at three – a quarter of the way around the clock face. It is a quarter past nine. We could also call this nine fifteen (9:15) because there are 60 minutes in an hour and so a quarter of an hour is 15 minutes.

Go to page 35

You grip the February handle and turn it. The door opens. You had remembered the old rhyme...

30 days hath September,
April, June and November,
All the rest have 31,
Saving February alone.
Which has but only 28 days clear
And 29 in each leap year.

You step inside, ready to face the burglars. Barkimedes is with you.

Go to page 37

You turn left and carry on. The light bulbs start to flicker – faster and faster. Then they go out! It is completely dark! You hear a deep growling sound ahead. Two green eyes appear from the shadows. What is it? From behind you comes a loud barking sound. The eyes back away.

You turn and follow your string back to the turning place. The lights come back on.

When you turned to the left you turned anticlockwise, . You should have turned clockwise, , and gone to the right.

Go to page 22

You lift down a cylindrical candle from the shelf. Its wick bursts into flame. The other candles start to light, too. The small room gets hotter and hotter! The candles start to melt – the flames start to spread!

You spot a bucket of sand in the corner. You spread the sand to smother the flames – that was close! You chose the wrong candle. A cylinder has two flat surfaces in the shape of circles – one at either end.

Go to page 15

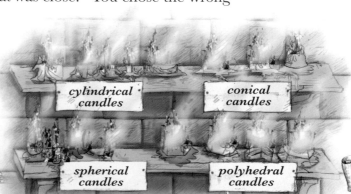

cylindrical candles

conical candles

spherical candles

polyhedral candles

You turn right and keep walking. The passage goes on and on. It's getting cold and damp. You shiver. Suddenly there is a scurrying sound. Something runs over your foot. There are rats down here, hundreds of them! They are biting at your trouser legs! Then something big jumps among the rats – barking and yapping. They scurry away.

You took the wrong passage! Perpendicular means 'at a right angle', or 90 degrees. You follow the string back to the turning point.

Go to page 12

You reach for the triangle-based pyramid. As you grasp it, the pyramid starts to glow. It's getting hotter and hotter! You can't let go! Sparks fly from its corners – your whole body starts to tingle and shake. Then something large leaps across the table, knocking the pyramid from your hand. Just in time – it explodes into a thousand pieces with a flash like lightning!

You chose the wrong shape. A triangle-based pyramid has 4 faces and 6 sides.

Go to page 30

That's the correct turret. You write 'south-west' in your notebook. You pick up the pyramid and head back to the Grand Hall.

Go to page 15

The January handle comes away in your hand! The door starts to shake. Smoke and flames spurt from the edges. Quickly you place the handle back in position.

How many days are there in January? How many in February?

January   February

Go to page 8

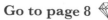

42

You've made half a turn. That's only 180 degrees! The pipes start to shake and squeal! You realize your mistake. You turn the wheel another half turn. That makes 360 degrees altogether. The pressure starts to fall.

Go to page 11

From inside the cupboard you hear the burglar's footsteps. Luckily he or she doesn't spot the broken loaf. You keep still until the footsteps retreat.

Go to page 9

There are three people in the room. A man and woman are standing. A second man is tied up in a chair. The two men look identical! At first the standing man and woman look shocked. Then the man tries to smile.

"Thank goodness you're here!" he says. "I am the owner of the Mansion and this is my cook. We caught the burglar and tied him up. He is my butler. He has disguised himself to look like me."

The woman smiles, she has a gap in her teeth! "That's right," she says. "He was about to get away. If you guard him, we'll fetch the police!"

Then the man in the chair speaks. "Don't listen to them," he says. "*I'm* the owner of the Mansion. I've been leaving you notes. These criminals are *my* butler and cook!"

Who should you believe? Then you remember the clues you have collected along the way. You ask the two men to hold out a hand and to take off a shoe. This is what you see...

standing man

sitting man

If you think the standing man is telling the truth, go to page 20

If you think the man sitting in the chair is telling the truth, go to page 32

Shape and measurement words

angle
Angles measure the amount by which you turn.

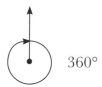

360°

A full turn is 360 degrees (360°).

180°

A half turn is 180°.

A quarter turn is 90°. This is called a right angle.

90°

The angle between two lines is the amount you must turn one to point in the same direction as the other.

acute angle

An acute angle is less than 90°.

obtuse angle

An obtuse angle is between 90° and 180°.

area
Area is a measure of the surface of a shape or an object. If the shape is drawn on a square grid you can find the area by counting the number of squares covered.

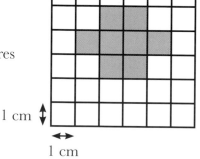

Area of shape = 8 square centimetres

1 cm

1 cm

circle

A circle is a perfect plane shape. Every point on its edge is the same distance from the centre. The distance from the centre to the edge is the radius. The diameter is the distance across the circle through the centre; it is equal to twice the radius. The circumference is the distance all the way around the circle.

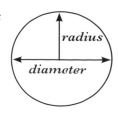

coordinates

Coordinates are numbers or letters that give the position of a point on a graph, grid or map. The first number or letter gives the position along the horizontal axis. The second number or letter gives the position along the vertical axis.

The coordinates of the point marked on the grid on the left are D,4.

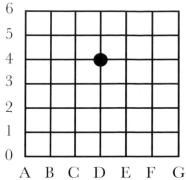

lines

A line is a straight or curved length with no width.
A straight line marks the shortest distance between two places. Parallel lines extend in the same direction. They are a constant distance apart and never meet – like the two rails of a railway track. Perpendicular lines cross at right angles.

parallel lines   *perpendicular lines*

measurements

Measurements are numbers that tell us the amounts or properties of the things around us. Your weight and height are measurements that tell you different things about your body. Other kinds of measurement include volume, time, area and temperature.

We measure mass in grams (g) and kilograms (kg). There are 1000 g in 1 kg.

We measure lengths in millimetres (mm), centimetres (cm), metres (m) and kilometres (km). There are 10 mm in 1 cm; 100 cm in 1 m; 1000 m in 1 km.

net

A net is a two-dimensional pattern for a solid shape. If you draw the net on card and cut it out, you can fold it to make the shape in three dimensions.

A net for a cube

plane shapes

Plane shapes are flat shapes you can draw on a sheet of paper. They are two dimensional. Triangles, circles and squares are plane shapes. Plane shapes made from straight sides are called polygons. Polygons are given names that indicate the number of sides. If all the sides are equal and all the angles are equal, the shape is regular.

Some plane shapes and their properties are given in the table.

Shape	Name	Number of sides	Special properties
	isosceles triangle	3	two equal sides and two equal angles
	equilateral triangle	3	all three sides and angles equal
	square	4	all sides equal and all angles right angles
	rectangle	4	all opposite sides equal and all angles right angles
	trapezium	4	two sides parallel
	pentagon	5	all sides equal on a regular pentagon
	hexagon	6	all sides and angles equal on a regular hexagon
	octagon	8	all sides and angles equal on a regular octagon

points of the compass

We use the points of the compass to give directions. A compass needle points north (N). The other cardinal (main) points are south (S), west (W) and east (E). We label directions half-way between the cardinal points as north-west (NW), north-east (NE), south-west (SW) and south-east (SE).

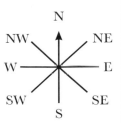

solid shapes

A solid shape is three dimensional; it has length, height and width. Spheres, cones, cylinders, cubes and pyramids are solid shapes.

sphere *cylinder* *cone*

A solid shape with straight edges is called a polyhedron. A cube is a regular polyhedron (all sides and angles equal), with eight edges and six faces. The names and properties of some different polyhedrons are shown in the table below.

Shape	Number of faces	Number of edges
cube	6	12
triangular prism	5	9
pentagonal prism	7	15
triangle-based pyramid	4	6
square-based pyramid	5	8

time

Time is the measure of interval between things happening – between the start and end of a TV programme for example, or between one birthday and the next. We measure time in seconds, minutes, hours, days, weeks, months and years.

60 seconds = 1 minute
60 minutes = 1 hour
24 hours = 1 day
365 days = 1 year (366 in a leap year)

We use clocks and watches to mark the passing of time.

Notes for parents and teachers

The Maths Quest series of books is designed to motivate children to develop and apply their maths skills through engaging adventure stories. The stories work as games in which the children must solve a series of mathematical problems to make progress towards the exciting conclusion.

The books do not follow a conventional pattern. The reader is directed to jump forwards and back through the book according to the answers they give to the problems. If their answers are correct, they make progress to the next part of the story; if they are incorrect the mathematics is explained, before the reader is directed back to try the problem again. Additional support may be found in the glossary at the back of the book.

To support your child's mathematical development you can:

• Read the book with your child.

• Solve the initial problems and discover how the book works.

• Continue reading with your child until he or she is using the book confidently, following the **Go to** instructions to find the next puzzle or explanation.

• Encourage your child to read on alone. Ask "What's happening now?" Prompt your child to tell you how the story develops and what problems he or she has solved.

• Discuss numbers in everyday contexts: shopping, filling up the car at the garage; looking at the car mileage and road signs when on journeys; using timetables; following recipes and so on.

• Have fun making up number sequences and patterns. Count in 2s, 3s, 4s, 5s and larger steps. Ask times-table questions to pass the time on journeys. Count backwards in different steps. List doubles, halves, square numbers and primes. Play "I'm thinking of a number, can you guess it?" games in which you ask questions such as "Is it even or odd?", "Is it bigger than 100?", "How many digits does it have?" and so on.

• Play number-based computer games with your child. The colourful graphics and lively animations will hold their interest as they practise basic number skills.

• Most of all, make maths fun!

start — —